I0006999

YOUR RIGHTS:

This book is restricted to your personal use only. It does not come with any other rights.

LEGAL DISCLAIMER

This book is protected by international copyright law and may not be copied, reproduced, given away, or used to create derivative works without the publisher's express permission. The publisher retains full copyrights to this book.

The author has made every reasonable effort to be as accurate and complete as possible in the creation of this book and to ensure that the information provided is free from errors, however, the author/publisher/ reseller assumes no responsibility for errors, omissions, or contrary interpretation of the subject matter herein and does not warrant or represent at any time that the contents within are accurate due to the rapidly changing nature of the Internet. Any perceived slights of specific persons, peoples, or organizations are unintentional.

The purpose of this book is to educate and there are no guarantees of income, sales or results implied. The publisher/author/reseller can therefore not be held accountable for any poor results you may attain when implementing the techniques or when following any guidelines set out for you in this book.

COMPENSATION DISCLOSURE: Unless otherwise expressly stated, you should assume that the links contained in this book may be affiliate links and either the author/publisher/reseller will earn commission if you click on them and buy the product / service mentioned in this book. However the author/publisher/reseller disclaim any liability that may result from your involvement with any such websites/products. You should perform due diligence before buying mentioned products or services

This constitutes the entire license agreement. Any disputes or terms not discussed in this agreement are at the sole discretion of the publisher.

Table of Contents

Introduction

There is a good chance you already have heard the buzzword and have a good idea about blogging or have even tried creating one for yourself. However, you still do not understand why everyone is so excited about having a blog and are willing to delve deeper into blogging. Makes you think, it has some form of magical draw you never got to enjoy.

The truth about this magical prowess is: blogging can make you rich! No kidding!

Blogging is simple to do. If you have created journals before, then creating blog posts should just be a walk in the park. However, blogging for the sake of doing it, is totally different from blogging to make a profit. What you're going to learn and discover in this e-book is the latter but I want to make sure you get the most out of your effort both as a creative outlet and as a viable cash-cow.

Here Is My Goal

When I started Internet marketing and blogging, I bought a lot of books. After all, you have to enrich your learning if you truly want to make it big in the writing-slash-information industry. However, e-books increasingly became more and more complex, for me, and I could no longer share them with friends who wanted to follow the same path of blogging success. I wish you all the success in the world. In order to increase your chances for success I am going to provide you with more free training.

My first goal, in creating this e-book is to lay out the information in the simplest way possible; no bells or frills. It is important for me, that once you have read the book, you will not feel like a newbie but more at par with an intermediate or even advanced blogger. In fact, I want you to start as a pro.

You will benefit from this report if you are:

✓ An Internet marketer ✓ A blogger ✓ A link building specialist ✓ An article marketer ✓ A digital product seller ✓ An affiliate marketer.

This way you will get the most out of your money-making opportunities.

You will also learn a lot about blogging, especially in the following areas:

✓ How to use blogging platforms in different ways than traditional blogging. ✓ How to use blog to promote your business. ✓ How to improve your blog's ranking.

✓ Various ways to make money through blogging. ✓ And ultimately, how to become richer through blogging.

Most of all, I will share secrets and tricks that you will not learn from anywhere else! Even the most seasoned bloggers like to keep these "secrets" under wraps! You will discover the ideal blogging platform for yourself, along with information on the various ways of monetization.

If you're expecting how to become a personal blogger after reading this book, you may be disappointed. You are not going to learn how to write personal reflections or how to upload photos and videos of your college ball. This e-book shows you how to bring in the profits with the least amount of effort as possible, with the help of great content and excellent promotional skills.

The New Media: Blogging

The truth is you will never learn how to blog with any success, until you teach yourself the principles and theories of modern blogging. In fact, you might never get to appreciate blogging in all its glory. So, before we move on to the techniques, let us talk briefly about what blogging is, and its many benefits.

What Is Blogging?

Many people believe that a blog (the shortened version of "web log") is just like a personal journal and just like them it permits the author to write about anything under the sun. The defining difference being, blogging has a worldwide audience. Some other characteristics unique to blogging include:

Open yourself to feedback

Blogs, typically have a feature where readers can share their thoughts and even arguments to your posts known as comments. It is one of the best ways of keeping in touch with your readers, customers and even potential clients. You can also instantly derive great ideas for your products and services that fit their niche or meet their needs.

Your blog can be shared

As long as you do not keep your entries private, other Internet users can share your posts or blog with their respective audiences.

A sense of organization

Blog posts can be classified in different ways: tags, keywords, categories, and date of publication, to name just a few.

Add media files

To encourage readers to visit the blog, a blogger can include media files such as images, videos, and audio files. This sort of technology cannot be integrated in a regular journal.

Write in reverse chronological order

This means newer entries appear first in the list. This is a huge advantage for Internet marketers e.g. for membership sites, members can access fresh content immediately after signing in. On the other hand, affiliate marketers can allow their readers to have first-hand information on product reviews once they load the blog.

Most of all...**Make money out of it**

Though journals like, "The Diary of Ann Frank" have grossed millions, it is not a likely outcome for most journals. Blogging, on the other hand, offers you unprecedented access to money-making opportunities. You

will learn a lot more about this lucrative aspect of blogging, as we delve further.

A Brief History of Blogging

There are two important stories that are related to the history of blogging.

First is its rise to popularity. Blogs are an inspired version of online diaries. As the popularity of Internet grew, it became a custom of many to create journals and keep track of their everyday lives through them; personal chronicles of sort! As new tools developed and platforms were created, blogging quietly and swiftly evolved to what it is today.

The word "weblog" came about around the end of 1997 and it was first used by Jorn Barger. However, it was Peter Merholz, who shortened it to the now famous "blog." You would be surprised to know, but blogging, as a trend started rather slowly until it picked up pace during 1999 and onward.

Before these blogs became so popular, there were already digital communities. You could describe them as a network of people who share opinions, thoughts, and, yes, stories! They would normally converge on platforms such as UseNet, e-mail lists, and Internet forums. They also made use of certain online services like CompuServe and Genie.

Benefits of Blogging

So why do people blog? Is it just because they want to share a part of themselves to the online community? Not everyone wants to earn money from blogging. Sometimes their main motivation for doing it is to simply talk about themselves and see how people react.

However, most people blog because they want to make a profit out of it in two ways: directly and indirectly.

An indirect way of earning money is through promotion. Let us say you have a business, and you want to develop your own brand and credibility. You use your blog to establish yourself as an expert in the field, bring your products and services much closer to your targeted audience, and allow them to send direct feedback to you.

You may also use it if you are an affiliate marketer. Most affiliate marketers such as Eric Holmlund of http://www.ericstips.com maintain websites on their own. This particular website has thousands of pages, and it would cost him good amount of money if he had to hire someone to update the content, but he made use of blogs to maintain such huge website with ease. (Eric is a super affiliate marketer, by the way. You can get heaps of great and very useful information about Internet marketing from him. Don't worry. He's also a cool guy. You can get in touch with him anytime you like by leaving your comments in his blog posts.)

When we speak of the direct method, it means the blog itself generates income for the blogger. Again, we will expound on these techniques later.

Just to give you a hint, though, the blog can carry ads paid by sponsors. Rumor has it that Perez Hilton, the owner of http://www.perezhilton.com, gets paid $9,000 for every ad.

Starting a Blog

Before you start creating a blog post, you need to have a blogging platform. This is a type of software that hosts or permits you to store your blog entries before they get published on the World Wide Web.

There are varieties of blogging platforms out there, thanks to the popularity of blogs. However, there are two general things you can do with them. You can have your blogs self-hosted or hosted.

The difference between the two

Let us define the two first. When you say self-hosted, it means that the blog is installed on your web host, and on your domain. e.g. http://www.yourdomain.com.

On the other hand, a hosted blog usually carries the extension of the platform used: http://iamasample.blogspot.com. Or http://iamasample.wordpress.com. This is because you allow the platform itself to host or take care of your own blog.

If you are going to choose between the two, it is best if you can have your blog self-hosted. Though it would mean additional cost for you since you need to pay for the webhost and the domain, it carries multiple benefits such as the following:

Blogs are favored by search engines

You need to have your blog indexed by search engines. Otherwise, it will be very difficult for your readers to find you. If you are trying to earn money, you want to drive as many people as possible to your blog.

Hosted blogs can still be indexed, however, self-hosted blogs are favored by search engines and get a better ranking too. This may spring from the assumption that those who spend money on their blogs are dead serious in creating blogs for the long-term. In turn, they avoid committing unethical practices that might compel search engines to ban their blogs.

More control over your blog.

You will still be limited to the tools and plugins available by the blogging platform, but you can have access to all of them unlike those who opt for hosted blogging. For example, if you self-host in LiveJournal, you can remove unwanted ads. You can add Google AdSense or any other advertising widgets in Wordpress, which you can never do if it is only hosted. You can also run other types of scripts. You can have as many pages as you want, as well as make use of plugins to better your search engine optimization (SEO) strategies.

More methods of earning

I have already mentioned Google AdSense. Now there are also blogging platforms that permit you to easily set up accounts with different affiliate programs. If you do not like to blog anymore, you can sell it to anyone who is interested and earn thousands of dollars out of it. Bankaholic was sold to BankRate for a staggering price of $150 million or $250,000 per page.

You can easily build your own brand. Self-hosting allows you to create your own domain name, which may be the actual name of your company or business. This way, it is much easier for your customers to remember your website.

Types of Blogging Platforms

As mentioned, there are many blogging platforms, but let us focus on the top 3 most popular ones:

Blogger
http://www.blogger.com

The first one is called Blogger. This used to be an independent one until it was purchased by Google. If you have a Google account, you can immediately sign up and start using it. You can get a Google account for free if you don't have one.

Blogger.com pales in comparison to other platforms when it comes to designer templates. Most of them are very common and bland, though new designs have been introduced lately. If you wish to add more eyecandy appeal to your blog, you have to be quite knowledgeable in CSS.

The main advantage of Blogger.com is that it integrates Google AdSense with ease, which is one of the easiest ways to make money for blogs. You simply have to set up a Google AdSense account and include the provided code into the template. You can then earn money every time any visitor clicks on the ads shown on your blog. Since it is powered by Google, it is easily indexed by the search engine.

You do not have to be a certified genius too to begin using Blogger. It has a very user-friendly layout page, where you can conveniently move your tabs and menus and create a somewhat different look for your blog. It has a WYSIWYG editor, which works very similarly to Microsoft Word. There are no issues attaching media files, from YouTube videos to your posts as well.

However, there are a couple of downsides. First, it is not too friendly with other type of plugins, simply because Google has produced their own for Blogger. There are restrictions importing external plugins to Blogger. For some strange reason, there are times when the pages are quite difficult to load. Blogger also deletes hosted blogs that are making use of automated software.

LiveJournal

http://www.livejournal.com

If you are looking for a no-frills blogging platform, this will be it. It started around the end of the 1990s and has gone through so many hands and companies, including Six Apart.

It has a user-friendly word editor. It permits users to create voice posts (or records of entries), and there are plenty of great templates to choose from.

You also have 5 different account levels, some of them are paid ones. Earlier, it was difficult to earn from the blogging platform until it gave the users the option to participate in its moneymaking program through Google AdSense.

You can also build a Friends' List and participate in Groups. This is ideal for Internet marketer since network connections help promote your business. Of course, you can create your own group and develop your own niche through LiveJournal.

However, it is not open to other external plug-ins. The sad thing is LiveJournal also has very limited plug-ins and tools you can use to further promote your website. Unlike Blogger, which is supported by Google, a huge search engine, it may take a while before a LiveJournal blog gets indexed.

WordPress

http://www.wordpress.com

Of all the blogging platforms out there, this is considered to be the best by many. In fact, many popular blogs make use of WordPress.

Sure, this also has many limitations. For instance, it is not that easy for you to customize CSS, though the number of themes you can choose have increased over the years. Unless you opt for a paid upgrade, it is difficult for you to earn money out of WordPress. You cannot settle for Google AdSense, text link advertising, and sponsored reviews. You are permitted to add only one link for your Amazon referral. It is so strict that violating a few terms on the TOS (terms of service) will mean automatic deletion of your blog.

However, WordPress also has a wide variety of plug-ins, which compensate for its limitations. Majority of them are available even for those who are using the blogging platform for free. For example, you can utilize Akismet, which is a default plugin, so you can trap spam comments. These types of comments can hurt your traffic and ranking in search engines.

You can easily integrate social networking widgets such as Facbook and Twitter. You can also set up a do-follow or no-follow plugin. This means those who want to link to your website can either benefit or not from your page rank.

The WP-DBManager, is another useful plugin that helps you create a backup for your WordPress blog. It also has an all-in-one SEO plugin and HeadSpace 2, which basically takes care of everything related to SEO.

SuperCache speeds up your blog by generating static html files of your blog. You can also make your weblog mobile friendly through WPtouch iPhone Theme.

With WordPress, you don't have to be a certified genius or a hard-core geek to set it up. The pages on your website do not need to be hand-coded, thanks to this dynamic CMS. You do not need to spend money on any programmer or website developer. You can update your very own blog without any extra help.

Setting Up Your Own WP Blog

I have been blogging for a lot of years and my experience has taught me two things: opt for a self-hosted blog and use the WordPress platform. This is what I am going to show you today.

Now, before we get into details on how to install your WordPress blog, you should know first how to choose the right web host. There are hundreds of them out there. In fact, it took me around 2 weeks before I found the right one.

It is not a good idea to just go for a cheap webhost. You want to know that your host company offers a good quality service and the tools you need to run your blog effectively. Some of the things you want to consider are:

Support

Your website may go down or face some issues. That's normal. What's frustrating is if it happens in the middle of the night, and there's no one to help you out. **Top priority:** pick a web host with a customer support available 24/7. No kidding.

It's also important; the person assisting you is accommodating, friendly and knowledgeable. It only adds to your disappointment if he or she is cold and doesn't posses the necessary skills to assist you solving your problem.

Easy WordPress Installation

If you are a newbie you might be a little bit nervous about using WordPress. But your web host actually holds the secret. They can provide you with a one-click installation through Fantastico. Fantastico is an easy to use add-on provided by the webhosts, which allows one-click installation of many open source applications including WordPress. You can also have full control over your weblog through its cPanel.

One of the common questions people ask me is this: what type of web host should I get? Better yet, what type of plan? Here's my suggestion, newbies. Go to http://www.hostgator.com.   They have one of the most comprehensive plans I've seen. I definitely love their baby plan, which guarantees unlimited domain, disk space, and bandwidth. There's certainly room for growth for your blog site.

It also has an SSL certificate, which means all types of payment transactions are secured. That's a big plus for Internet marketers since buyers would definitely like to protect their confidential information such as their name and credit card number. If this isn't enough, you can get the plan for less than $10 a month.

What to Do with Domains

Of course, you can never have a blog without a domain. Consider it as your own address in cyberspace. Like your personal home address, you want it to be easily remembered and spelled out for friends and guests. You also want to keep it very short.

There are many places where you can buy your domain, which you can own for a year. Many would recommend GoDaddy, but I seriously suggest you don't. The problem comes in when you're accused of spamming and then the registrar deactivates your domain and steals it from you when it's not your fault, or if you can prove you are sending legitimate emails. No one had recourse.

There's tough competition there, and you'll get better support and service from other places such as http://www.namecheap.com. A domain will cost you around $10 a year, but if you're resourceful enough, such as looking for coupons in Google, you can reduce the price to almost $2.

Installation of WordPress

There are two ways to install WordPress: manually and a one click process through "Fantastico De Luxe". Manual Installation is a very long process and a little complicated leaving room for error. That is why I suggest you choose to use Fantastico.

Here's what you're going to do:

Step 1:   Sign up for a web hosting account. I already provided you with the guidelines as well as the best website to go to for the plan.

Step 2:   Once you have a web hosting account, you'll be provided with the username and password. You can use the information to log in to your cPanel. At this point, open your cPanel.

The URL of your cPanel will be www.yourdomain.com/cpanel

Step 3:   Look for the "Fantastico De Luxe" icon. Make sure that the web hosting account offers you this feature. Some don't, and you need to purchase it. That's going to be costly at your end. The icon, by the way, is the one with a smiley face.

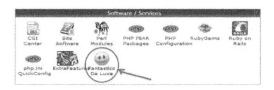

Step 4: Scroll down until you get to the Blogs section. Among the list, choose
WordPress by ticking the button.

New Installation (2.8.4)
Disk space required: 9.04 MB
Disk space available: 996382.5 MB

Current installations:

Step 5: At the right-hand side, you will see information about
the type of WordPress you're going to install. It's important
that you get the latest version. Otherwise, refer the issue to your
web host. If everything is okay, press New Installation.

Step 6: You will then be redirected to the one-click installation
process. This includes determining the Installation Location,
Admin Access Database Configuration, and E-mail Account
Configuration.

Make sure you can leave the Installation Location blank if you
want the weblog to be your main page. If not, create a folder that doesn't
exist yet. This is where you're going to install all information about your
weblog.

23

The Admin Access Data is the area where you're going to create the username and password for your WordPress.

Base Configuration contains the details related to your blog, such as your nickname or username. You can be very creative about it, but it's best if you stick to your own name. This is the name that appears on every blog entry and reply you make on the comments. You will also create the name and description of your blog. Again, you can be artistic, but it's recommended you include targeted keywords or related description to your blog.

You don't have to set up the E-mail Account Configuration if you're not planning to blog through your e-mail.

Step 7:   Press Finish Installation. You will then receive a notification confirming the successful setup of your WordPress blog.

Tweaking WordPress Setup

Is it enough that you installed WordPress? The answer is no. You need to do some tweaking for a number of reasons. First, you want your weblog to rank in search engines, else, there's no traffic for your blog. You have to be friendly to the Internet users too. If they don't like your blog, don't expect them to visit you again.

You don't have to be a Superman when you're tweaking. Start with the basics.

Permalinks

Change the permalink structure. Permalink means permanent link. This means it doesn't change. If the page gets indexed, it's the link that is cached. Natural permalinks are composed of a series of characters—numbers and letters—that are unreadable. The default WordPress permalink looks like http://yourdomain.com/?p=ID. That's why they are not considered user as well as search engine friendly.

The good news is you can change the permalink structure. The bad news is doing this after a while is not ideal since issues will surely arise, such as wrong redirection.

To set up your permalink, go to WordPress Admin -> Dashboard -> Options -> Permalinks. Select Customize Permalink Structure.

In my opinion the best permalinks options are:

/%category%/%postname%/
or
/%postname%/
or
/%postname%.htm

Embed Media

Include media files. I for one don't love to check weblogs that are based on text only. They remind me of the physics and chemistry books back in college. Entice your readers and expound your thoughts by adding media files, such as images, videos, and audio. Here are instructions for you: http://codex.wordpress.org/Using_Image_and_File_Attachments.

Add a theme

The theme adds aesthetic value to your blog. You can just imagine a wall. You will be attracted to one that has more colors and designs than to something that's just plain white.

WordPress already has plenty of themes to choose from. To access them, open your account, go to your dashboard, click on Appearance, and select Themes.

Here's the downside, though. As mentioned, you cannot change them easily if you not a tech savvy. If you want something more personalized, you have to opt for a paid theme. For starters, though, just select any of the available themes on the website.

Plug-ins

I could never stress this enough. WordPress has become so flexible because of the plug-ins, and there are far too many to cover everything here. So let's start with at least five. For me, they are also the most essential ones.

Make sure you can install them in your WordPress account even before you start creating your blog post.

Akismet (http://wordpress.org/extend/plugins/akismet/) – This is a plugin that traps spam comments. You don't want them in your website. Moreover, visitors hate spam, and they view any website with lots of it as completely unprofessional.

Google XML Sitemaps

(http://wordpress.org/extend/plugins/googlesitemap-generator/) – What's a sitemap? It's simply a place where you can find all the pages on your weblog. That's also the place spiders crawl in, searching for pages to be indexed. If you want your blog to be friendly to search engines and have as many pages indexed as possible, then you have to install Google XML Sitemaps. You can control the URL, date of crawl, and other important information.

Google Analytics (http://wordpress.org/extend/plugins/google-analyticsfor-wordpress/) – This is one of the most important tools for Internet marketers. The bottom line of creating a weblog is to earn profits.

However, you will never get to that point if you don't understand your visitors in the first place.

Google Analytics helps you with that. It tells you how many visitors are going to your website, which pages are checked, what types of keywords are used to find your blog/pages/posts, how long they stayed etc. They are useful because they help you in your marketing campaigns. It will help you understand if you're driving the right types of people into your weblog, if the keywords are working well for you, or if you're getting the right click-through rate for your weblog.

WP Super Cache (http://wordpress.org/extend/plugins/wp-super-cache/)
– You need this to load your pages faster. In case you didn't know, Internet users stay for a very short time on any website. If it doesn't load within 10 seconds, expect them to leave and never come back.

All-in-one SEO Pack (http://wordpress.org/extend/plugins/all-in-oneseo-pack/) – Don't stress yourself when it comes to SEO. This is your ultimate superhero. It improves and optimizes titles, meta tags and is designed to be compatible with WordPress e-commerce websites.

Making Money: Stop The Adsense

When I made the decision to earn money through blogging, there was only one strategy I had in my mind: AdSense. During that time, everyone was doing it. I had friends who never stopped yapping about their $100$300 earnings every month. I thought, "Well, okay, if I can just write and write and set up the ads, then perhaps I can earn twice as much. Even if I don't succeed, then $600 isn't that bad after all. I can use it to pay for the mortgage."

Well, I was wrong. AdSense took a lot of effort at my end it's actually hard to earn as much as my friends. Worse, many Internet users had become so unattached to them they don't click on the ads anymore!

So I figured, "If I'm dead serious about earning through blogging, then I have to find new ways." I did. This is what I'm going to share to you: how to get past the AdSense hype and earn real income.

Selling Products and Services

One of the most effective means of earning through blogging is selling products and services. These products and services can be physical or digital. Take a look at the examples below:

Physical Products

- Health and wellness products
- Toys
- Gifts
- Apparel
- Home Improvement
- Collectibles

Digital Products

- E-books
- Software
    - Applications
    - Games
    - Even Services like Coaching, Graphic designing etc.

You get the idea.

Anyway, the best thing about selling a product or a service is you can have a very close idea of how much you're going to earn. After all, these things have their own fixed prices. It's easy for you to expand your goods so you can touch on more niches. For example, in the area of home improvement, you can now sell environment-friendly furniture and fixtures for earth-conscious customers. You can upsell and cross-sell. Moreover, as long as you can provide great service to your customers, they will stick with you.

However, before you can actually start selling items, you need to accomplish a very important thing: A Sales Page.

The sales page doesn't sell the products per se. For the customers to buy the items, they have to proceed to your website, go to the Shopping Cart, place an order, and pay through whatever means is shown on the shopping cart. But your sales page is fundamental since it's your come-on page, the one that tells your leads why it's a good idea to buy items from you.

This is where majority of Internet marketers and sellers fail. They just don't know how to do it. You may be a good writer when it comes to writing your own sales letter in a notepad or word document, but if you don't know how to make html page, those efforts will be completely futile.

The good news is WordPress makes it so much easier for you (see, I just love WordPress!). You can simply install a plug-in that helps you turn your page into a sales page.

You can then simply copy and paste your copy as a regular post and place an order link of the product you're selling. Once the customer clicks on it, he or she will be redirected to a payment processing page, where he or she can place an order and pay.

You can also choose among the paid plug-ins available. Now before you complain about spending more, you should know how powerful they are:

Salespage Plugins

http://easywpsalespages.com/ - This is perfect for people who lack visual abilities. You don't have to think about how to format your sales page as this product carries multitudes of in-built designs you will be done with your sales page in minutes (true). There is also a variety of cutesy and colorful Add to Cart buttons just to enhance the aesthetic appeal of your page.

http://www.flexsqueeze.com/category/squeeze-pages/ - There are fewer templates to choose here, but what it lacks in number it makes up with its design. Theirs are truly professional looking. What's more, they are categorized according to the type of call to action or message you want to send to your potential customers. Moreover, the sales page can also function like a blog, so you're hitting two birds with one stone with this one. Take note, though, that the price can be very hefty. It costs more than a hundred dollars.

http://www.wpsqueezepage.com/ - It produces very neat sales page, easy to install, quite cheap at $47, and doesn't give you any headache during

customization. However, this doesn't work in any of the templates of FlexSqueeze.

You can also check out other great choices:
http://creationspire.com/wpspire/ (for more advanced Internet marketers) and http://www.wordpressppc.com/

Quick Tips

Because of the many options and the possibility of marketing with great ease, it's so easy for you to get caught up or feel overwhelmed by the numerous tools available. It's more convenient for you to play with the designs. However, it's the content that matters. Do take time to learn how to write a good and compelling sales copy. It's not possible for me to cover copywriting here, so if you want to learn just look around your competition or search Google for good converting sales pages.

Here are few tips for you to begin with:

- Know the audience. When you know who you are selling too, you can set the right tone.

- Add magic words. You can always get the attention of Internet users when you have "free," "secret," and "top product," among others, in the title or anywhere in your sales letter.

- Include testimonials. If you've gone through beta testing, add the reactions or feedback to further strengthen the claims you've made.

- Focus on the benefits. People are interested in products they need. So you need to answer the question "What's in it for me?" in your sales page.

- Go for facts. Back up your claims with proven research, and don't say anything you cannot substantiate later.

Affiliate Marketing

When I decided to earn money seriously through blogging, this was the field that I got into. And so far, I have never regretted this. One of the things I love about affiliate marketing is I don't need to have any product of my own or keep any inventory. I don't have to be mindful of any physical orders. However, I can still be a salesperson—and a good one at that.

For those who aren't familiar with affiliate marketing, let me provide you with some background. An affiliate is someone who is connected to a much bigger entity. For example, I could be an affiliate to Dresses.com, which sells gorgeous gowns. Anyway, but that doesn't mean I am a fulltime employee of the organization. I earn through commissions and other methods of earning, including fixed rate or percentage of sales.

For me to start earning, though, I need to promote the products of the said company. That's what affiliate marketing is all about.

You may ask, though, "How does affiliate marketing relate to blogging?" In fact you can even ask how it works together with WordPress. I'll tell you how.

The Power of the WordPress

There are at least three important things you should do when you're doing affiliate marketing:

- Build your credibility
- Attract potential customers

- Promote products and services

All these three you can accomplish when you create a blog through WordPress.

First, you need to build your credibility. Otherwise, no buyer is going to click on your affiliate link and buy something through your weblog. It's in the same way you don't just buy stuff on eBay unless you've read all those user reviews of the seller.

But how do you build credibility? Through your blog posts and comments, of course! You can write some really good content on regular basis that will prove your level of knowledge and expertise about the subject. Okay, let's make use of the same example above with Dresses.com. If you want to truly sell, you may want to feed your potential customers information on how to pick the right product for them. You can also guide them on what colors or trends are considered in season, as well as how they can improve their look through accessories.

You can also send your reply to all those who give you feedback via comment form. Now, you cannot expect all of them to say just nice things about your data or even about you. It's time to prove to them that you're a professional affiliate marketer by how you deal with those negative criticisms. I for one would love to deal with businesspersons who know how to handle issues and complaints so well.

Second, you attract potential customers by the types of subjects you write about. So many affiliate marketers rely on targeted keywords when they create topics for their audience.

If you want to join the bandwagon, you can go to https://adwords.google.com/select/KeywordToolExternal. This is a good idea especially when you are starting out.

However, you should also learn to be more in tune or observant of the industry you're in. Sometimes tools won't tell you that "2010 trends" are commonly searched, but you may just want to write something about it as many of your readers will be interested.

You can also give away plenty of freebies too: e-books, free subscription to your newsletter, tools, or even a sample of what you're trying to sell to them. You can actually increase your click-through rate to as much as 12% if you have something to give away.

WordPress also permits you to install social network plug-ins such as Facbook (http://wordpress.org/extend/plugins/wp-facbookconnect/) and Twitter (http://wordpress.org/extend/plugins/twitter-tools/).

This way, all those who are in my Facbook and Twitter Friends' list can receive instant updates and can also view and send comments about my entries. Simply put, you spend less time on creating your affiliate site and more time promoting.

Of course, the main reason why you're doing all this is because you want to sell. Fortunately, it's actually very easy when you're doing with WordPress, you can immediately add a link to your affiliate site. Here's an example: "Get the dresses that fit you so well and make you look gorgeous by visiting http://myaffiliatelink.com"

Important Tips:

- Do check out again the blog http://www.ericstips.com/ to get heaps of tips on affiliate marketing, especially if you're starting out.

- Don't forget to add your affiliate link in your post. Make sure it works too.

- If you don't have any account with affiliate programs yet, open an account at http://www.clickbank.com. It's the best so far in the industry. What's more, registration is completely free.

- Write a blog post, even a short one, at least three to four times a week.

- Try cloaking the link. Thieves are also abundant, and they are out there to steal your affiliate link. In the end, it's them who get the commission out of your own personal efforts, not you. However, here's a great news. You can install the plug-in from http://www.mbpninjaaffiliate.com/ so you can cloak your links instantly.

- Never, ever forget to create an affiliate disclaimer. It is in compliance with FTC. You can read more about it here: http://izea.com/ftc-compliance-easy. Just to give you an overview, you should make sure that your readers know that the links found on your website are affiliate links and you are compensated promoting the product. Not having one may just get you in a legal mess.

Review Sites

You can turn your WordPress into a review site. What does this mean? It's similar to affiliate marketing but this one is more dedicated and provides details about the product and it's competition. Review sites convert very well because the visitor doesn't have to do much research, as it's already done by the reviewer (that's you!)

All you have to do is to deliver your expert opinion about it. It's one of the best ways to earn money because writing reviews enhances your credibility. Combine this with affiliate marketing, and you can expect your conversion rate to increase to several folds.

Tips

- You may want to use this plug-in:

http://wordpressreviewplugins.com. It greatly improves your review by allowing you to create comparison tables, import information from any kind of database, develop star ratings, and can work with any WordPress theme.

- Gather as much information as you can. Your reviews should not be based solely on mere opinions. You need to provide your review with the facts. If you can, interview experts, read journals, and watch videos provide your own screenshots, photos etc..

- Be honest. There's no other way to be trusted than that. Honesty is important because your customers are not going to come back if you have misled them in any way. If you recommend a product that doesn't really work, you're damaging your name and the product you're selling. Heck, you may even find yourself in a lawsuit.

Membership Sites

There are two important questions that need to be answered about membership websites:

Why should you opt for content management system? Why should you use WordPress?

Why content management system?

The main motivation for Internet users to sign up for membership website is they want to have access to exclusive information. So far, the best type of presenting information out there is through a content management system. With it, you can easily add new content, rearrange them, and combine various media files: texts, videos, and audio.

You can also easily manage the content. You can add, modify, or delete content and you don't have to be a programmer or an HTML expert to do that. It's the same thing when it comes to features as well as your list of members. It also encourages interaction among members through feedback forms. They may also add one another as friends.

Why WordPress ?

Based on my experience, WordPress offers great flexibility managing content and there are quite a few good plugins that can turn your WordPress CMS into a full-fledged membership site while protecting your members only content.

Protecting your content is the utmost priority if you are running membership websites. The entire program is useless if the public gets to see the information. These plugins permit you to protect premium posts with a lot of additional flexibility.

Just to give you an idea what they are, check out some examples below:

WishList Member

(http://wordpressmembershipplugins.net/wishlist-member/) – It is very easy to install, and offers the following: download protection, payment system, content delivery, partial content protection, autoresponder integration, protected RSS feeds, affiliate program, and available membership levels.

It also offers extensive customer support and 30-day money-back guarantee

Members Only

(http://wordpress.org/extend/plugins/members-only/) – It helps control the posts that are meant to be exclusive. Posts remain hidden unless the Internet users signs up or logs in.

HidePost

(http://wordpress.org/extend/plugins/hidepost/) – It hides certain aspects of the posts. Only the members can have full access to them.

User Access Manager

(http://www.gm-alex.de/projects/wordpress/plugins/user-accessmanager/) –

It gives you a lot of freedom on how you want to manage user access and the membership website.

You may also visit http://www.ryanlee.com. This guy maintains a membership website through a blogging platform.

Lead Generation

If you're an Internet marketer, you don't promote your product to just about anyone. You have to determine your market and attract the right people into your business. These are the potential customers to whom you're going to sell.

WordPress can also be a very effective tool for lead generation. First, as you've learned a few pages earlier, there are so many themes that will allow you to build your squeeze or landing pages on the fly. You can also come up with a variety of them with various subscription forms depending on the submission habits of your Internet users. Most definitely, there is a bunch of themes you can use, some of them available here: http://www.squeezetheme.com

Traffic Generation

When you're in cyberspace, traffic takes a whole new meaning. It's common for people to get irked when they're stuck in traffic, but it's something you look forward to when you're in the World Wide Web.

Traffic means people, but they are not just any Internet user. These are the ones who visit to your weblog, read your posts, click on your affiliate links, and purchase your products. They are the ones who will refer your weblog to their friends and family, create reviews about your business, and just basically become a walking-talking ad. They are your network connection. Without them, your business will die—and I'm sure of it.

There are plenty of conventional methods of driving traffic into your blog:

- Article marketing
- Forum marketing
- Blog marketing
- Link building
- Social networking
- Directory submission

These are techniques that I use when I promote my blogs. They do work, no doubt, but they also take so much of your time. For instance, if you want to do article marketing, you have to write at least a 300-word article, which will take you around 30 minutes. Then you have to submit the

article to various article directories and wait for around 24 to 48 hours before you will know if you get approved or not.

So what I'm planning to show you is how you can drive traffic to your website with the least amount of time possible. You can do these through a number of plug-ins you can install into your WordPress blog:

Tell-a-friend

(http://wordpress.org/extend/plugins/search.php?q=tell+a+friend) - Tell a Friend allows your Internet user to share the blog post or the weblog to their friends and family. Another script you can use is http://plugins.trac.wordpress.org/wiki/wp-email. But what I like about Anup Raj's plug-in is you can conveniently customize it.

Digg Integrator

(http://bill2me.com/digg-integrator/) – Digg has thousands of subscribers all over the world, and they are very active. When you become part of Digg, your posts can be reviewed, shared, and rated by the rest of the members of the website. With the integrator, Internet visitors who have Digg accounts can just click on the buttons, and your post can then be posted into their respective profiles.

The good news is you can customize the appearance of the buttons, so they can add more appeal to your blog.

Chicklet Creator 2

(http://www.twistermc.com/social-bookmark-plugin/) – Okay, I do recommend that you integrate as many social networking websites as possible. However, one of the biggest problems I faced was they overcrowded my weblog! It's a good thing I found this social plug-in.

Popular social networks are just in the drop-down menu, de-cluttering your pages.

Other Plug-ins:

- Google Analytics http://wordpress.org/extend/plugins/googleanalytics-for-wordpress/
- Subscription Options http://wordpress.org/extend/plugins/subscription-options/
- Keywords Plug-in http://vapourtrails.ca/wp-keywords
- Social Traffic Monitor http://wordpress.org/extend/plugins/socialtraffic-monitor/

Content Is King

These tools can only do so much for you. If you don't have great content, nobody wants to read your posts, or share them with others. So take your time when you create a blog post. Make sure it's original, timely, easy to read and understand, free of grammatical errors, precise, and engaging.

Don't forget to add a call to action too, perhaps telling the readers to download something or buy your product and service. Promote your affiliate and product links whenever you can in every post.

Blogging Techniques - Not

Everyone Knows

Perhaps you're one of those who have downloaded quite a few blogging e-books, so you feel like you know everything you need to know about the subject. Well, you can be wrong. I did that too, and so far, I discovered that virtually all of them fail to talk about or recommended the following tips I want to share with you.

Here are some of the blogging techniques not often discussed:

LSI Keywords

LSI stands for latent semantic indexing. Sounds complicated, right? Not really. It simply means using other related terms to the main keyword all throughout the article.

It's a common knowledge that to rank highly in your targeted keyword, you have to reach a specific keyword density. This means you have to use the keyword quite a number of times in the article, say, 3 to 5 times depending on the density you are aiming for and the length of the article.

However, Google changes algorithms frequently, and today they prefer those articles that sound more natural. That's why it's recommended you use LSI keywords.

To help you understand it a lot better, let's pretend you're selling toddler toys. Instead of repeating the same phrase many times, you can use "toddler toys for sale," "toys for kids, "how to buy toys for kids," etc.

To know more about LSI, visit http://www.inlineseo.com/blog/2008/10/22/lsi/

Live Blogging

I have to tell you honestly that I am not such a great fan of live blogging, since I can have a very short attention span sometimes, but it's one of the best ways of getting traffic into your site today.

Live blogging simply means posting notes and media files in real time. You may be invited to a press conference or a trade fair, and you blog everything that's happening. Usually, blog posts in live blogging are very, very short.

They attract traffic because admit it people want the freshest news and scoop. What else could be newer than sharing something that's still happening, right?

Live blogging doesn't have to be too complex. You can use tools such as http://www.coveritlive.com and http://wordpress.org/extend/plugins/liveblogging (this one is for WordPress bloggers). You can also use your dependable Notepad if you wish to share some items not covered during your live blogging.

Advanced Blogging

Why should you do this? Shouldn't you blog in a timely manner? Well, you might not want to blog all of the time. Sometimes you're stuck with other important commitments, or you're going on a very long vacation, and your spouse is making it clear you're not going to do anything with your business or blog.

So you do advanced blogging. This is quite different from creating drafts because with drafts you still have to manually publish them. In advanced blogging the posts get published automatically at your designated time.

Thanks to Wordpress, this is going to be so easy:

1. Create your blog post.
2. Locate the Post Timestamp.
3. Edit the information by clicking on Edit Timestamp.
4. Determine the time and date of publication.
5. Press Publish.

Feed Burners/ RSS Feeds

What are RSS feeds? RSS stands for Really Simple Syndication. What it does is it publishes the content of your weblog to the websites and blogs of your subscribers. This way, they don't have to check on your blog at all times. They can also receive the most up-to-date content.

There are different types of feed burners or RSS Feeds websites you can use. One of these is Google Feedburner. Because it's from Google your feed also gets easily indexed and faster.

Another option is http://wordpress.org/extend/plugins/copyfeed/, which allows you to add a copyright message to your feeds.

Conclusion

Based on a survey conducted by Technorati in 2008, more than 90 percent of blogs are left to become idle—not earning money though possibly gaining visitors. However, as long as your blog remains not updated, you cannot expect these Internet readers to hang on for a long while. They will soon leave, and the blogs are left to "die."

There are many reasons why people leave their blogs. However, two of the foremost are the lack of motivation and the difficulty of maintaining the blog.

Everything I discussed with you today hopefully changed your mind-set about blogging. You don't have to be an ordinary blogger. Most of all, you don't have to earn pennies when you can earn hundreds to thousands of dollars every month through your blogs.

If you're not fully motivated by money, then surely you will feel inspired by the hundreds of people who follow you, those who look up to you for comments and suggestions, those who are willing to share their thoughts and put their trust in your credibility and level of expertise.

The various plug-ins and tools you can utilize when you're blogging will make things so much easier for you too. Yes, you don't have to be the most hi-tech WordPress blogger in the world. You simply need to know which tools or plug-ins to use to maximize the power of your blog and convert it into your ultimate profit machine.

I will be creating step by step videos showing you exactly how to create, setup and monetize a wordpress blog as well as getting free and low cost traffic to it.

To get access to the FREE Wordpress Website Install and setup video just go to http://www.ultimateblogincomesystem.com/blog and learn how to install and setup your wordpress website.

Here is another training course book I wrote called: "How

To Make Money Online: Doing what You Already know and love"

You can check it out at the link below:

http://www.amazon.com/How-Make-Money-Online-Alreadybook/dp/B019NIJNIY

If you are interested in learning How To Become A Super Affiliate Marketer I have created a system that willl show you how to sell your own or other peoples products online.

I have been an affiliate marketer for about 5 years now and have made a fantastic living selling other peoples products as an affiliate and I did it using Wordpress Blog Websites.

I wish you all the success in the world. In order to increase your chances for success I am going to provide you with more free training.

When you signup here→Register For The FREE Money Making Training

You will receive 3 more guides over the next 7-10 days
PLUS video training to visually teach you some tactics and
techniques to create an online business.
I will also be doing live webinars where you can ask me
questions (I usually charge $250.00 per hour just
for this)

.

Get the free report "Super Affiliate Survival Guide " Here and learn
some tips and tricks to create a massive income online.

Here are some of my other Internet Marketing Training Systems
that I will provide to you FREE to help you make money online:

**Article Marketing Training- Use articles to get free traffic to your
website**
Kindle Edition

Make More Sales Online - Using Social Media For Internet Marketers
Kindle Edition

The Super Affiliate Marketing System- How To Sell Other Peoples Products Kindle Edition

Author is avaiable for private and group coaching, seminars and speaking engagements at kbjunor@gmail.com.

I wish you all the success in the world. In order to increase your chances for success I am going to provide you with more free training.

When you signup here→Register For The FREE Money Making Training

You will receive 3 more guides over the next 7-10 days PLUS video training to visually teach you some tactics and techniques to create an online business. I will also be doing live webinars where
you can ask me questions (I usually charge $250.00 per hour just for this)